T0006196

She
Persisted

··

RACHEL LEVINE

··

—INSPIRED BY—

She Persisted

by Chelsea Clinton & Alexandra Boiger

. . . .

RACHEL LEVINE

. . . .

Written by
Lisa Bunker

Interior illustrations by
Gillian Flint

PHILOMEL

PHILOMEL BOOKS
An imprint of Penguin Random House LLC, New York

First published in the United States of America by Philomel Books,
an imprint of Penguin Random House LLC, 2023

Text copyright © 2023 by Chelsea Clinton
Illustrations copyright © 2023 by Alexandra Boiger

Visit us online at PenguinRandomHouse.com.

Library of Congress Cataloging-in-Publication Data is available.

Printed in the United States of America

HC ISBN 9780593529034
PB ISBN 9780593529041

1st Printing

LSCC

Edited by Talia Benamy and Jill Santopolo.
Design by Ellice M. Lee.
Text set in LTC Kennerley Pro.

∽ Dedicated ∾
to all young rainbow humans everywhere.
Dare to dream! The world is lucky to have you.

Dear Reader,

As Sally Ride and Marian Wright Edelman both powerfully said, "You can't be what you can't see." When Sally said that, she meant that it was hard to dream of being an astronaut, like she was, or a doctor or an athlete or anything at all if you didn't see someone like you who already had lived that dream. She especially was talking about seeing women in jobs that historically were held by men.

I wrote the first *She Persisted* and the books that came after it because I wanted young girls—and children of all genders—to see women who worked hard to live their dreams. And I wanted all of us to see examples of persistence in the face of different challenges to help inspire us in our own lives.

I'm so thrilled now to partner with a sisterhood of writers to bring longer, more in-depth versions of these stories of women's persistence and achievement to readers. I hope you enjoy these chapter books as much as I do and find them inspiring and empowering.

And remember: If anyone ever tells you no, if anyone ever says your voice isn't important or your dreams are too big, remember these women. They persisted and so should you.

Warmly,
Chelsea Clinton

She Persisted

She Persisted: TEMPLE GRANDIN

She Persisted: DEB HAALAND

She Persisted: BETHANY HAMILTON

She Persisted: DOROTHY HEIGHT

She Persisted: FLORENCE GRIFFITH JOYNER

She Persisted: HELEN KELLER

She Persisted: CORETTA SCOTT KING

She Persisted: CLARA LEMLICH

She Persisted: RACHEL LEVINE

She Persisted: MAYA LIN

She Persisted: WANGARI MAATHAI

RACHEL LEVINE

TABLE OF CONTENTS

....

....

Nature vs. Nurture

How much are we already ourselves when we are born, and how much are we shaped by the people who raise us? This is called the question of nature vs. nurture. Nature is how you are born, and nurture is the care that shapes you. Different people have different answers to this question, but most people agree it's some of both.

When Rachel Levine was born in 1957 in a quiet suburb in Massachusetts, there were already many things that were true about her.

One was that she was born into a family of hardworking lawyers. Her mom and dad both practiced law. This was back when lawyers were mostly men, so Rachel's mother was a pioneer.

Another thing that was true about young Rachel was that she had curly blond hair. She was also very smart, and as soon as she started school, she loved it and was good at it.

And Rachel was born transgender, or trans for short. That means that she was born with a boy body, but on the inside, in her mind and in her heart, she was a girl.

The first time that Rachel knew for sure that she was a trans girl was when she was five years old. She was reading a story in a comic book about a superhero named Superboy. In this particular

story, an alien woman from another planet used a magic ring to turn Superboy into a girl. When Rachel read that, she knew that that was what she wanted and needed too.

There were two problems, though. The first problem was, it didn't seem possible. The magic ring wasn't real.

The second problem was, she didn't know how to say what she wanted, to another person or even to herself. In those days, hardly anyone knew anything about transgender people. Most of the words for talking about trans people hadn't been invented yet. And there were hardly any real examples in the world. There was no one Rachel could point to and say, "I'm like her."

So Rachel compartmentalized. That's a long word, but it's easy to understand. A compartment is a place to store something away. Rachel took the knowledge that she was a girl and hid it away in a secret place in her brain.

Then she did her best to act like a boy. She did a good job, and most of the time she didn't mind doing it. It felt OK to play a boy in the world, at least for the time being. It was easy, because everyone already thought she was one. But whatever she was doing, in her mind she could see herself doing the same thing as the girl she knew she was.

Rachel had a happy childhood. She played with her big sister, Bonnie, and the other kids on her street. There were fun summer vacations on Cape Cod. Rachel joined her dad in being a fan of Boston sports teams. And she got to see her mom making her way as a strong woman in a

world of work run almost entirely by men.

Rachel's parents loved her and took good care of her. They showed her by the lives they lived that it was important to work hard and to help other people. She liked those ideas and took them as her own. That's an example of how nurture matters just as much as nature.

From the beginning, Rachel was also the sort of person who, when people asked her to do something, she almost always said yes. She liked making other people happy, and she liked being part of what was going on around her. Was that nature or nurture? Probably some of both.

When she was still quite young, Rachel discovered a love of science. One of her early dreams was to be a geneticist—someone who studies how traits are passed from parent to child—so she learned as much as she could about genes and heredity. But as she got a little older, the dream changed to being a doctor instead.

Rachel learned other things too. For example, she took a class to learn to speed-read, and then she had a skill that helped her do her homework faster.

She also took a class at a gym to learn to fight. She did that because she thought that since she was acting as a boy in the world, it was a skill she needed to have. That class didn't help her as much as the speed-reading class. What she learned in fight class was that she didn't want to fight.

A less pleasant thing happened as Rachel grew older: she was bullied at school. You might think it was because she was transgender, but it wasn't. She was still compartmentalizing and acting the role of a boy, so no one knew. She was bullied because her family was Jewish, and because both of her parents worked.

The answer Rachel's parents came up with to the bullying problem was to move her to a private school. They hoped that there, she would thrive.

The Torpedo

Belmont Hill School was a private high school for boys. When Rachel was a student there, she still knew that on the inside she was a girl, but she wanted to fit in, and she still had no idea how to actually change and become the girl she knew she was. So she kept on acting the role of a boy in the world.

The regular kind of acting—being in school plays—was one of several things Rachel was interested in in high school. She also played football and hockey, and sang in the glee club. And she worked hard and did well in her classes, especially biology.

By the time she was close to graduating, she was working each summer in a nearby medical lab, learning how to help with research. She had set her feet on the path to becoming a doctor, and she took every opportunity that came her way to learn what she needed to achieve that goal.

Rachel worked so hard and did so well at Belmont Hill School that she got into Harvard University. Harvard is one of the oldest and most famous colleges in the United States. It is also one of the toughest.

In her first few years at Harvard, Rachel continued to act in plays, but after a while she had to stop because her schoolwork demanded all of her time. Even though she could speed-read and had been teaching herself all her life how to work hard, she found her classes challenging.

At Harvard, Rachel was still thinking all the time about being a girl. In the Harvard library, she went looking for books to help her, but the books she found were no help. They were written by people who didn't understand what trans meant. The books told Rachel that she was crazy.

Rachel knew that she wasn't crazy, but she still didn't know how to show the world who she really was, so she kept on compartmentalizing and acting.

There are many steps to becoming a doctor. After you graduate from college, the next step is medical school. Rachel graduated with honors from Harvard and then went to Tulane University in New Orleans, Louisiana.

In medical school, you have to decide what kind of doctor you want to be. There are many, many choices. At Tulane, Rachel discovered that she enjoyed treating children, especially teenagers. There was a new idea at that time that there could be a kind of medicine just for teenagers, called adolescent medicine. Rachel decided that that was the kind of medicine she wanted to practice.

The other students in the school called Rachel "the Torpedo." They called her that because she just kept going and going, no matter what.

At Tulane, Rachel also met and fell in love with a girl named Martha. At the end of medical school, Rachel and Martha got married.

Then it was time for the next step on the way to becoming a doctor, called a residency. A residency is when you are a doctor-in-training at a hospital. Residency work is famously hard. In Rachel's first year of residency, she had to work for thirty-six hours at a time without stopping, two or three times a week.

Can you imagine working for thirty-six hours without stopping? That means getting up in the morning, working all day, then on into the evening and all through the night without sleeping, and then working all the next day too, before you could finally go home and go to bed.

Rachel's residency in adolescent medicine was at Mount Sinai Hospital in New York City. Martha was doing her own residency in the city at the same time. They both worked so hard

that they never used the kitchen in their tiny apartment, even though they lived there for years.

After Rachel's residency was over, Rachel

and Martha worked for five more years in New York City. Rachel was happy in her work and doing well, but the city was a hard place to live. It cost so much money that even two doctors could only have a small apartment. Rachel and Martha were planning to have children soon. They needed more room.

So they decided to make a change. They moved away from the city and found new jobs in the state of Pennsylvania.

·····························

Responsibility and Transition

In her new job in Pennsylvania, Rachel was more than just a doctor. She was also a teacher, a researcher, and an administrator. An administrator is someone who helps run things.

But that's not all. Rachel was also an innovator, someone who makes new things happen. She started an adolescent medicine program, and once it was going, she ran it. She also started a program for young people with eating disorders, which are mental illnesses that cause people to make unhealthy choices about food. She worked with doctors in other departments, and once the program was running, she was the boss of that too.

And, on top of all that work, Rachel and Martha had two babies. David was born in 1994 and Dana was born in 1996. Maybe people didn't call Rachel "the Torpedo" anymore, but she still deserved the name. She had many responsibilities, and she worked hard all the time to meet them.

She didn't mind. In fact, she liked it. But there was something else going on at the same time as all that hard work. As Rachel got a little older, her feelings about really being female got harder to compartmentalize. She found she couldn't push them away anymore.

So Rachel made room in her busy life to spend a little time taking care of herself. She found a therapist to help her figure out what to do. The therapist asked her an important question. He said, "If you could wave a magic wand and make these thoughts and feelings go away, would you do it?"

At first Rachel thought, *Of course I would,* but then she thought about it for a few days more. She went back to the counselor and said, "No, I wouldn't make the thoughts and feelings go away. They are part of who I am."

The counselor said, "OK then, let's explore the possibilities."

Rachel began to educate herself. She learned that there are many trans people in the world, and that if they want to, they can switch from living the way the world has told them to live

to living as their true selves. This is called going through gender transition.

Some trans people transition all at once, but Rachel chose a different path. She decided to change gradually and see where it led.

She let her hair grow out. She started wearing women's clothes, just a little bit at first, then more and more. When people noticed and made comments, she made jokes about being a bit of a hippie, a flower child from the 1960s.

Rachel was finally letting herself be the person she knew herself to be. Finally, the images she had always had in her head of herself as a girl and woman could become her reality.

Rachel's long, slow experiment with change continued for several years, until the change had happened. She had switched to living as a woman in the world. She didn't have to compartmentalize or act anymore. She could just be.

It felt so good to be her real self at last, and most of the people in her life accepted her. The hardest part was that Rachel's wife was uncomfortable with the change. Rachel and Martha's marriage ended, but they stayed good friends.

Rachel's children accepted her. Her mother said, "I figured something was up. You're wearing nail polish and women's clothes. I don't understand, but I love you no matter what."

That made Rachel so happy that she cried. It can be scary telling someone you love about such a big change. There is always a chance that they might reject you. But that didn't happen to Rachel, and she knew that she was lucky.

Rachel was aware that some people lost

their jobs when they transitioned. Not Rachel. She figured out ways to help the other people at her job understand and accept her transition. Her co-workers liked her and liked working with her, because she was so responsible and helpful and kind. That made it easier for them to accept her.

Rachel might have spent the rest of her working life as a doctor and teacher and administrator, but one day she got an unexpected phone call.

Public Health

The phone call that changed Rachel's life was from the governor of the state of Pennsylvania. He called to invite her to become the physician general of Pennsylvania. The physician general is the chief doctor of the whole state and gives the governor advice about health and medicine.

The governor had thousands of doctors to choose from. Why did he call Rachel? He found

out about her because of work she did with Equality Pennsylvania, a group that fights to protect LGBTQ+ people—those letters stand for "lesbian, gay, bisexual, transgender, and queer"—in the state. In other words, it was because she had found yet another way to be helpful.

When the call came, Rachel said yes right away, even though it meant that she wouldn't be able to see patients anymore. Her new kind of work, making medical decisions for a whole state, was called *public health*. Rachel felt a little sad to be giving up treating patients one at a time, but she understood that by moving into public health, she could move from helping people one at a time to helping all of the people in an entire state.

First, though, she had to be accepted for her new job by the state senate. That might have been tricky, because there are some people in the world who think transgender people are crazy or dangerous.

Trans people are not crazy or dangerous. They are just regular people who happen to have a mismatch between their bodies and who they know themselves to be on the inside. But not everyone understands that.

Even though some of the senators might have had wrong ideas about trans people, they did still decide that Rachel should get the job. They agreed that she should serve because of all the hard work she had done and all the experience and knowledge she had.

Rachel's new job was important enough that it was reported in the news. At first the news reports talked about the fact that she was trans, because it was new to have a trans person in such an important and powerful position. Not all of the reporting was kind. Rachel just kept working, and after a while the news stopped talking about her gender and just reported on what she was doing.

There are many people who have never met or heard of a trans person, so just by showing up for work every day, Rachel was teaching everyone around her that trans is normal and healthy. This is called *representation*, and it's important. She taught people to pay attention to what she was doing, not her gender identity. In this way she was a pioneer, like her mother.

One of the worst problems that many people in Pennsylvania were facing when Rachel became physician general was drug addiction. There are powerful drugs that people use in ways they shouldn't, without a doctor helping them. Sometimes people can't stop taking them even if they want to, and sometimes they take too much and die from overdoses.

When someone is having an overdose, they can be saved if they get another medicine, called naloxone, right away. A few minutes can make the difference between life and death. Rachel thought that it would be a good idea if first responders like police officers and ambulance crews could carry some of this life-saving medicine with them.

To make that happen, she had to get a lot of people to agree that it was a good idea. She also had to make sure that her idea wouldn't get the state of Pennsylvania in any kind of trouble with the law.

Just like she always had, she got to work. She convinced all the right people that her idea was a good one. She talked to lawyers to make sure it was a safe idea. In the end she was able to write a standing order for naloxone.

It was like a doctor writing a patient a prescription to get medicine at the pharmacy, but for the whole state. It meant that police officers and ambulance crews everywhere in Pennsylvania could get as much naloxone as they needed to help people who were having overdoses.

Many first responders took advantage of Rachel's standing order, and they started saving people. Rachel's standing order has helped first responders in Pennsylvania save more than two thousand lives.

As physician general of Pennsylvania, Rachel

also fought for the rights of LGBTQ+ people, studied how diseases spread from one person to another in the state, and asked questions about how people in the state were getting cancer. She was invited to speak everywhere around the state, and she always said yes.

She gave lots of speeches, representing as she went. She figured out every way she could to be a good top doctor for Pennsylvania, and she was helping more people than ever before. But more changes were on the horizon.

CHAPTER 5

Bigger Stages

After a while, Rachel's boss, the Pennsylvania secretary for health, decided to go back to being a doctor, and Rachel was asked to take over the job. Of course she said yes, just like she had her whole life long.

Now she found herself in charge of a huge statewide agency, trying to make the state a healthier place to live. Because she kept saying yes, she kept finding ways to help more and more people.

Shortly after she became secretary for health, the COVID-19 pandemic began. COVID was the biggest health emergency in the United States since anyone could remember, and as health secretary, Rachel was what she called "the point of the spear" in Pennsylvania. She started posting videos online every day, telling people how to keep themselves and their families safe from this dangerous new disease.

COVID was a scary and complicated problem, and many people had strong feelings and different ideas about what to do about it. Some of the people who watched Rachel's videos attacked her online. Some of the attacks were about science and medicine, but some were about the fact that she was trans. People posted awful comments and sent her hateful messages.

Rachel couldn't let that happen without doing something. She added an extra speech at the start of one of her daily briefings. In her speech she told the people who were attacking her that they weren't attacking just her. She said they were attacking everyone who is LGBTQ+. "We have not made progress unless we have all made progress," she said.

She also said she had no use for hate. "My heart is full with a burning desire to help people, and my time is full with working towards protecting the public health of everyone in Pennsylvania . . . and I will stay laser-focused on that goal." Fewer people attacked her online after that, because she stood up for herself so well.

One morning in 2021, Rachel woke up to a text that had come to her phone overnight. It was from someone who worked for Joe Biden, who had recently been elected president of the United States. The text asked if Rachel would be interested in switching from doing public health work for Pennsylvania to doing it for the whole United States of America.

By now you know that of course Rachel said yes to this new opportunity too. She was offered the position of assistant secretary for health for the entire nation.

The process for taking this new job was even more complicated than when the governor of Pennsylvania called about working for the state. First Rachel had to be vetted, which means being asked a lot of questions and having the government go back through all your history, looking for things that might be a problem. All they learned about Rachel when they vetted her was that she wanted to help people and that she worked really hard.

She also had to be confirmed again, this time

by the US Senate. She had to go and answer questions face-to-face with senators on national TV. A few senators asked her rude and ignorant questions about trans people, but Rachel kept her cool and answered by talking about public health.

In the end the Senate voted fifty-two to forty-eight to confirm her as the United States' new assistant secretary for health. Rachel was the first trans person ever in the history of our nation to be confirmed by the Senate for such an important job.

The work she did in her new position was like the work she had been doing before in Pennsylvania, but on the national stage. Now she was boss to six thousand people, and the decisions she made affected everyone in the whole country.

The United States was still fighting its way

through the pandemic. She helped with that. She also worked on drug addiction and overdoses again, and studied ways to make sure everyone in the country could have a fair chance to get help from a doctor if they needed it.

Every day, the work she did made life better for people all over the country. She helped our nation be a safer and healthier place during a very difficult time.

· ·

High-Water Marks

O ver the years, because of all her hard work, Rachel had been given various awards and honors. Of course it felt good when that happened, but they were not the main reason she did what she did. Remember what she said about laser focus. For Rachel, the work was always about helping people.

There was one big honor that came with Rachel's new position that did make her very happy. As assistant secretary of health, she was allowed to choose to become an officer in the United States Public Health Service Commissioned Corps, which is one of the eight uniformed services in the United States.

Rachel was given the rank and the uniform of four-star admiral. At her swearing-in ceremony, Rachel gave another speech. She talked about how her father and two of her uncles had served in the armed forces during World War II, and about how she was following in their footsteps.

She also said, "I am honored to serve as the first female four-star officer of the US Public Health Service Commissioned Corps, and the first openly transgender four-star officer to serve across any of the eight uniformed services . . . I stand on the shoulders of those LGBTQ+ individuals who

came before me, both those known and unknown. May this appointment today be the first of many more to come, as we create a diverse and more inclusive future."

Because of her new job, sometimes Rachel was invited to the White House. She got to meet President Biden several times.

One time at an event, someone who was giving a speech said something nice about Rachel, and people started clapping. President Biden told her to stand up so that everyone could see her. Can you imagine having a job where the president tells you to stand up to be recognized? Wouldn't that be amazing?

When people talk about how progress gets made, sometimes they use the image of waves on a beach. If you've ever been at the beach when the tide is coming in, you know that the waves climb higher up the sand. Not every wave goes higher, but if you wait long enough, another big one will come and reach higher than any wave before. People call that a new high-water mark.

On her way to becoming one of the nation's top health officers, Rachel made several high-water marks, both as a woman and as a trans person. She showed the world that transgender people can help millions if given the chance. She fought hard to make the world a safer place for LGBTQ+ people, and just by being herself she taught the world that trans people are good and kind and normal.

Rachel Levine started out as a secret girl who wanted to help people, who was willing to

work hard, and who said yes when people asked for help. Some of that, especially her gender identity, was how she was born, and some of it was how she was raised.

But whatever the exact mix of nature and nurture, what was most important about how she lived her life was that she stayed true to herself. She knew who she was and what she wanted to do. She set her feet on the path toward her goals, and then she worked as hard as she could for as long as she had to to reach those goals.

It wasn't always easy. Sometimes the path forward was hard to find, like when she was going through her long, slow gender transition. Sometimes people reacted to her and to her work with hate. But she just kept going.

Rachel Levine has dedicated her life to the

common good, and no matter how hard the work was or how mean people were, she has persisted. She has shown the world that trans women can be leaders and champions. She is the torpedo who became an admiral.

HOW YOU CAN PERSIST

by Lisa Bunker

Here are some ways to honor Rachel's persistence and to learn from the example of her life:

1. See if you can find a seed inside yourself of caring about other people, and then ask yourself, *How can I make this seed grow?*

2. Challenge yourself to work harder than you think you can. The next time you are working on a difficult task, when you get to the point where you think you need a rest, try to keep going a little longer.

3. When someone asks you to help with something, try to say yes, even if you are not sure it is something you will like or be good at. Then stick with it until the task is done.

4. If you are not trans yourself, find some more stories about transgender people and learn about their lives. Then, if you hear someone say something

wrong or mean about a trans person, speak up. This is called being an ally, and it is a powerful way to help.

5. If you are trans yourself, once you know you are ready and it feels safe, express your gender truth and live your authentic life proudly!

6. If someone you know ever tells you that they are a different gender than you thought they were, believe them, and use whatever name and pronouns (like she, he, they) they ask you to use.

7. Research the different kinds of doctors there are, and see if you can decide

which one you would choose to be if you were in medical school.

8. Tell your friends and family about what you've learned about Rachel Levine, and be ready to educate them about what it means to be trans if they need that help.

⟡ References ⟡

Bunker, Lisa. Interview with Admiral Rachel
Levine. March 28, 2022.

Loveland, Barry. "LGBT Oral History: Rachel
Levine." LGBT History Project of the LGBT
Center of Central PA, February 6, 2017.
archives.dickinson.edu/sites/all/files/files_lgbt
/LGBT-interview-transcription-Levine-Rachel
-064.pdf.

"Pennsylvania Health Secretary Dr. Rachel
Levine responds to acts of LGBTQ,

transgender harassment." YouTube, uploaded
by 6abc Philadelphia, July 28, 2020. youtu.be
/3D9FxzbvNYU.

"Rand Paul questions Rachel Levine on gender-
affirming care for minors." YouTube, uploaded
by *Washington Post*, February 25, 2021.
youtu.be/Krf0Cm-FKro.

"Swearing-in of Dr. Rachel Levine to the U.S.
Public Health Service Commissioned Corps."
YouTube, streamed live and uploaded by US
Department of Health and Human Services,
October 19, 2021. youtu.be/psZiJhwAVO4.

Dr. Levine Coronavirus Update

SUBSCRIBE

UP NEXT

LISA BUNKER (she/vo/they) is the author of *Felix Yz* and *Zenobia July*, two novels for young readers featuring LGBTQ+ main characters who are regular kids with strengths and flaws, just like everyone else. From 2018 to 2022 she represented the town of Exeter in the New Hampshire House of Representatives, as one of the first out trans state legislators in US history. Lisa is married and has three grown children. Her many interests include chess, birding, playing the bass, gender, story craft, and language. In 2022, she moved from New Hampshire to Sacramento, California.

Photo credit: Melissa Koren Photography

You can visit Lisa Bunker online at
LisaBunker.net
or follow her on Twitter
@LisaBunker

GILLIAN FLINT has worked as a professional illustrator since earning an animation and illustration degree in 2003. Her work has since been published in the UK, USA and Australia. In her spare time, Gillian enjoys reading, spending time with her family and puttering about in the garden on sunny days. She lives in the northwest of England.

You can visit Gillian Flint online at
gillianflint.com
or follow her on Twitter
@GillianFlint
and on Instagram
@gillianflint_illustration

CHELSEA CLINTON is the author of the #1 *New York Times* bestseller *She Persisted: 13 American Women Who Changed the World*; *She Persisted Around the World: 13 Women Who Changed History*; *She Persisted in Sports: American Olympians Who Changed the Game*; *Don't Let Them Disappear: 12 Endangered Species Across the Globe*; *It's Your World: Get Informed, Get Inspired & Get Going!*; *Start Now!: You Can Make a Difference*; with Hillary Clinton, *Grandma's Gardens* and *Gutsy Women*; and, with Devi Sridhar, *Governing Global Health: Who Runs the World and Why?* She is also the Vice Chair of the Clinton Foundation, where she works on many initiatives, including those that help empower the next generation of leaders. She lives in New York City with her husband, Marc, their children and their dog, Soren.

You can follow Chelsea Clinton on Twitter
@ChelseaClinton
or on Facebook at
facebook.com/chelseaclinton

ALEXANDRA BOIGER has illustrated nearly twenty picture books, including the She Persisted books by Chelsea Clinton; the popular Tallulah series by Marilyn Singer; and the Max and Marla books, which she also wrote. Originally from Munich, Germany, she now lives outside of San Francisco, California, with her husband, Andrea, daughter, Vanessa, and two cats, Luiso and Winter.

You can visit Alexandra Boiger online at
alexandraboiger.com
or follow her on Instagram
@alexandra_boiger

Read about more inspiring women in the

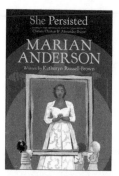

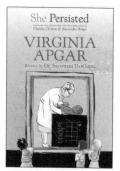

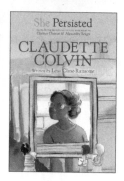

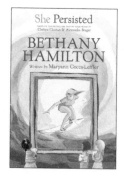

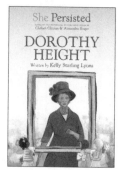

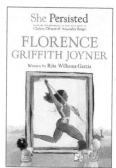